POETRY STARS

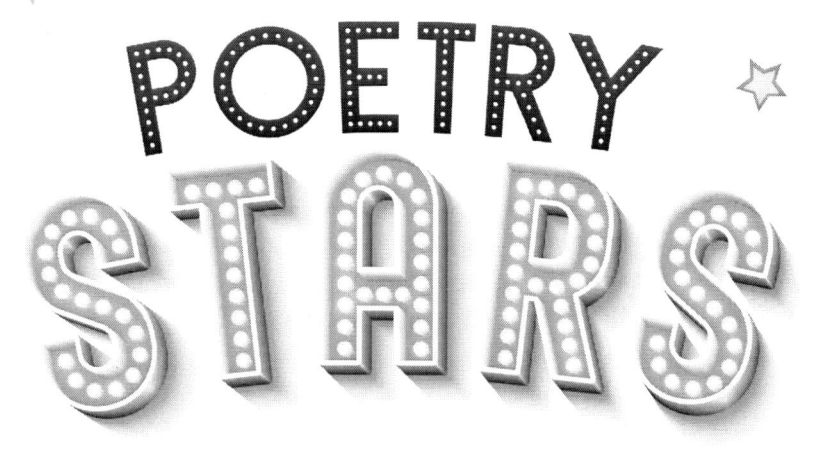

Amazing Poets

Edited By Byron Tobolik

First published in Great Britain in 2023 by:

YoungWriters®
Est. 1991

Young Writers
Remus House
Coltsfoot Drive
Peterborough
PE2 9BF
Telephone: 01733 890066
Website: www.youngwriters.co.uk

All Rights Reserved
Book Design by Ashley Janson
© Copyright Contributors 2022
Softback ISBN 978-1-80459-342-4

Printed and bound in the UK by BookPrintingUK
Website: www.bookprintinguk.com
YB0530E

FOREWORD

Welcome to a fun-filled book of poems!

Here at Young Writers, we are delighted to introduce our new poetry competition for KS1 pupils, Poetry Stars. Pupils could choose to write an acrostic, sense poem or riddle to introduce them to the world of poetry. Giving them this framework allowed the young writers to open their imaginations to a range of topics of their choice, and encouraged them to include other literary techniques such as similes and description.

From family and friends, to animals and places, these pupils have shaped and crafted their ideas brilliantly, showcasing their budding creativity in verse.

We live and breathe creativity here at Young Writers – it gives us life! We want to pass our love of the written word onto the next generation and what better way to do that than to celebrate their writing by publishing it in a book!

Each awesome little poet in this book should be super proud of themselves, and now they've got proof of their imagination and their ideas when they first started creative writing to look back on in years to come! We hope you will delight in these poems as much as we have.

CONTENTS

Belvoir Park Primary School, Belfast

Robbie Boal (8)	1
Naomi Murray (11)	2
Harry Dolan (9)	3
Kaitlyn Barkley (8)	4
Charlie Mccleery (9)	5
Harley Griffiths (9)	6
Niamh Murray (11)	7
Max Moore (9)	8

Chantry Middle School, Morpeth

Grace Brown (9)	9

Edward Wilson Primary School, Westminster

Issra Nader (9)	11
Carmen Chan-Naylor (9)	12
Mohamed Kouira (6)	13
Salma Youssef (8)	14
Rehab Abdellah (9)	15
Aseel Khan (7)	16
Janna Merza (8)	17
Uzma Qazizada (9)	18
Hussain Al-Ansari (10)	19
Zaynab Jannah (9)	20
Alaya Haque (6)	21
Yasmin Saemh (6)	22
Adyaan Ali (6)	23
Diletta Vannone (6)	24
Sania Habib (7)	25
Ahmad Al Salhani (7)	26

Greenside Primary School, Pudsey

Casey Broadbent (6)	27
Ophelia Meegan (5)	28
Joss Mottram (5)	29
Edie-Rose Horman (5)	30
Alfred Butterfield (5)	31
Valentina Haigh Del Rio (9)	32

Hallglen Primary School, Hallglen

Jessica Marszol (7)	33
Mudassir Khan (7)	34
Eloise Fraser (7)	35
Harris Conroy (7)	36
Sophie Winton-Love (7)	37
Matthew Fyall (6)	38
Logan Neary (7)	39

Jesmond Gardens Primary School, Hartlepool

Max Parkinson (6)	40
Chloe Parkinson (10)	41
Shay Malham (8)	42
Leon Foster (11)	43
Callan Simpson (10)	44
Hollie Bradshaw (8)	45
Octavia Trainer (7)	46
Daniel Shaw (10)	47
Emmie Pearce (7)	48
Dean Malham (6)	49

Marshgate Primary School, Richmond

Molly Conneely (8)	50
Charlie Sheldrick (8)	51

Nelson Primary School, Ladywood

Eva Kuzmina (6)	52
Amna Abdulwhab (5)	53
Amelia Vrapi (6)	54
Namarikh Isak (6)	55
Marina Ago (5)	56
Fareda Elshafey (5)	57
Karen Ireoluwa Taiwo (6)	58
Sama Arjah (5)	59

Seahouses Primary School, Seahouses

Jaxon Appleby	60
William Armstrong (5)	61
Daisy Winter (5)	62
Arthur Priestley (7)	63
Jacob Rowe	64
Veronika Karpyshyn	65
Luella Campbell (6)	66
Sophie Bolam	67
Reggie Stanwix	68
Jessica Owens	69
Ava Thompson	70
Paige Douglas	71
Sienna Robinson (7)	72
Luke Liddell	73
Alfie Neale	74
Nela Skibicka	75
Delilah Dunn	76
Layla Kidd	77
Milana Filonenko (7)	78
Leo Wood	79
Lailie Nakintije	80
Axel McGilligan (6)	81

South Rise Primary School, London

Michael-Junior Cameron (5)	82
Summer-Lilly Eldridge (6)	83
Romziyah Yusuff (5)	84
Noah Assimeng-Boahene (6)	85
Asma Derder (5)	86
Esma-Nur Sasmaz (6)	87
Kaelin Pun (5)	88

St Aidan's Catholic Primary Academy, Ilford

Aaron Singh (10)	89
Sarab Sahota (10)	90
Deivan Virdee (10)	92
Eunice Bonanga (10)	93
Pedro Ekemezie (10)	94
Destiny Ugwu (10)	95
Safiyya Moosa (10)	96
Isabella Jackman (10)	97
Ariana Zaman (10)	98

St Mary's Lewisham CE Primary School, Lewisham

Sarai Mallett-Odeyale (7)	99
Ananya Vijithan (7)	100
Elyas Yahya (7)	101
Eddy Charles (7)	102
Haja Jalloh (7)	103
Temi Adelaja (8)	104
Lucian Stefan Eftimie (7)	105
Sandra Aguilera (7)	106

Stonesfield Primary School, Stonesfield

Megan Ivanov (9)	107
Iris Maroney (10)	108
Imogen Doucas (10)	110
Billy Hulusi (10)	111
Daniel Hunt (9)	112
Tegan English (10)	113

Abel Stuart (9)	114
Leo Turner (10)	115
Aaliyah Gregory (9)	116
Isaac Smyth-Medina (10)	117
Rocco Hulcup (10)	118
Leland Edwards (9)	119
Daniel (10)	120
Rowan Ball (11)	121
Freya Harris (10)	122
Ellis F (10)	123
Samuel Smith (9)	124

The Bemrose School, Derby

Tayabung Rai (7)	125
Princess Adetoyese (6)	126
Amy Nirmal (6)	127

Willington Prep School, Wimbledon

Jonas Full (5)	128
Angus Timlin (5)	129
Alexander Hohlfeldt (6)	130
William Parkhouse (5)	131
Edward Lu (5)	132
Matthew Plant (5)	133
Reuben Stern (5)	134
Charlie Livesey (5)	135
Maxim Russell-Omaljev (5)	136
Tom Fell (5)	137
Edward Jones (5)	138

Yeading Infant & Nursery School, Hayes

Rishi Sivathasan (6)	139
Khushleen Kaur Bhogal (6)	140
Saim Hussain (6)	141
Riyana Chudasama (6)	142
Taimur Nizam-Uddin (6)	143
Zorawar Buttar (6)	144
Harleen Gill (6)	145
Harjot Singh (6)	146

Aya Al-Hulu (6)	147
Ranveer Singh (7)	148
Akshaana Parthipan (6)	149
Maisa Azad (6)	150
Eshan Rekhi (6)	151
Israr Ahmed Shinwari (7)	152
Harleen Jaspal (6)	153
Sahib Gill (6)	154
Shay-Anne Kirk (7)	155
Abhishaek Rajeswaran (6)	156
Jasreet Khabra (7)	157
Akai Nithiyaramnarayanan (6)	158

Yelvertoft Primary School, Yelvertoft

Jessica Dymond (10)	159
Reuben Flavell (10)	160
Niamh McElfatrick (9)	161
Elijah Elliott (9)	162
James Fleming (9)	163
Kirin Kaur Madhar (9)	164
Eva Newhouse (9)	165
Tessa Clews (10)	166
Natalie Ritchie (10)	167
Tommy Starkey (10)	168
Grace Micklewright (11)	169
Bethany Shaw (9)	170
Elouise Shakespeare-Luck (10)	171
Matilda Kington (10)	172
Flynn Armstrong (9)	173
Esme Carter (9)	174

THE POEMS

Robbie

R unning Robbie
O utside, playing with friends
B lue is my favourite colour
B usy playing on my PS4
I play Fortnite
E ating pepperoni pizza.

Robbie Boal (8)
Belvoir Park Primary School, Belfast

An Autumn Walk

I can see my horse getting his winter coat.
I can hear birds singing.
I can feel that the tree is cold.
I can taste blackberries.
I can smell hot chocolate.

Naomi Murray (11)
Belvoir Park Primary School, Belfast

Harry

H appy Harry
A lways playing Lego
R ascal
R ed is my favourite colour
Y esterday, I saw King Charles III.

Harry Dolan (9)
Belvoir Park Primary School, Belfast

An Autumn Walk

I can see leaves.
I can hear birds singing.
I can feel seed pods popping.
I can taste blackberries.
I can smell crab apples.

Kaitlyn Barkley (8)
Belvoir Park Primary School, Belfast

An Autumn Walk

I can see Max.
I can hear birds singing.
I can feel seed pods popping.
I can taste blackberries.
I can smell crab apples.

Charlie Mccleery (9)
Belvoir Park Primary School, Belfast

An Autumn Walk

I can see leaves.
I can hear birds singing.
I can feel the sun.
I can taste blackberries.
I can smell wet leaves.

Harley Griffiths (9)
Belvoir Park Primary School, Belfast

An Autumn Walk

I can see a dog playing with a ball.
I can hear a dog panting.
I can feel blackberries.
I can taste berries.

Niamh Murray (11)
Belvoir Park Primary School, Belfast

An Autumn Walk

I can see sticks.
I can hear the water moving.
I can feel seed pods popping.
I can taste blackberries.

Max Moore (9)
Belvoir Park Primary School, Belfast

My Class

My class, my class, my class,
Better than the rest,
My class, my class, my class,
Just the best.

Like a shooting star in the night sky,
Across our delicate book,
Our pencils fly,
It could make you shook.

The teacher paces,
Back to the right,
Like cars in races,
A shot of light.

When we talk,
And someone's sad,
We make them happy by,
Being *mad!*

My class, my class, my class,
Better than the rest,
My class, my class, my class,
Just the best.

In class,
We do do things wrong,
Like whispering,
Or singing a song.

My class is the best,
My class is better than the rest.

Grace Brown (9)
Chantry Middle School, Morpeth

Meeting My Bestie!

As I entered the store,
I found a puppy staring at me with joy,
It wagged its tail and jumped up and down,
Every time I took a step closer.
As Mum was checking the price,
I looked around the store,
It was a farm-like place.
Cats meowing, dogs barking,
Birds tweeting and hamsters squeaking.
The puppy looked like a white cloud
On the ground, the price was £300.
I thought it was cheap,
But Mother looked at me with a grin and
said, "Oh darling, you have more to learn."
I carried my puppy home and said,
"You are my new animal friend!"

Issra Nader (9)
Edward Wilson Primary School, Westminster

Butterflies

1, 2, 3, you can count on me,
How many butterflies can you see?
Colourful wings everyone loves,
Don't get me confused with a pair of gloves.

They can be blue or sometimes pink,
Some of them are family, so they link.
Bodies as skinny as a pen,
I didn't know some of them were men.

Wings as big as a bottle cap,
Sometimes they land on your lap.
Most butterflies don't live very long,
So if you see one, sing them a song.

Have you seen a butterfly?
Was it as beautiful as the night sky?

Carmen Chan-Naylor (9)
Edward Wilson Primary School, Westminster

Amazing Antarctica

A ntarctica has emperor penguins and king penguins
N o people live there because it's freezing
T he Terra Nova once took Edward Wilson
A ntarctica had active volcanoes
R ight at the bottom of our planet
C oldest place on Earth
T he biggest desert in the world
I n summer, it always stays light
C an you imagine going to Antarctica?
A ntarctica surrounds the Southern Ocean.

Mohamed Kouira (6)
Edward Wilson Primary School, Westminster

All About Pancakes!

P ancakes are great, they make us feel happy!
A lways eat pancakes because they are delicious
N ever eat anything except pancakes
C an't live my life without pancakes
A pancake smells like creamy vanilla frosting
K ittens don't like pancakes!
E verybody in the universe should like pancakes
S ome people don't like pancakes but we can try to make them like pancakes.

Salma Youssef (8)
Edward Wilson Primary School, Westminster

O' Summer

O' summer,
How the smell of beautiful flowers comes to your senses,
When roads and crowds are all tense.
O' summer,
Taking the last quiz,
Tasting how ripe the honey is.
O' summer,
Now there is the sun,
That's when you know it's time for fun.
O' summer,
Going on holiday,
Once you get to the airport, it feels like a runway.
O' summer.

Rehab Abdellah (9)
Edward Wilson Primary School, Westminster

Hoop It Up!

H ula hoop is swinging around my waist
U nder my hips that are swaying away
L illy, my sister, hula hoops her breath away
A nother day in May, Lilly will be found

H ard at play
O ne day, children were lined up like troops
O n a sunny day, watching Lilly use that
P owerful strength and hula hoop away.

Aseel Khan (7)
Edward Wilson Primary School, Westminster

Poem About My Mother

My mother is the best,
She never ever rests.
She works hard, day and night,
To make my future very bright.
She teaches me new things every day,
And there is always time to play.
She is like a teacher to me,
That is why I am not afraid to be me.
One day, when I grow up,
I would like to thank her for never giving up.

Janna Merza (8)
Edward Wilson Primary School, Westminster

Pandora (Avatar)

Mythical, marine bushes staggering beneath the trees,
A life of paradise for the mythical creatures,
Eye-catching reptiles run around fantasy trees,
Immortal plants sprout out like perfectly watered flowers,
Dream-like fish swim around the futuristic pond.

Uzma Qazizada (9)
Edward Wilson Primary School, Westminster

Shackleton

If he can go to Antarctica,
Why can't I?
He has dreams,
So do I,

He is strong,
So am I,
He's an explorer,
Me too

He has a crew,
My friends are my crew,
He has a boat,
I can buy one too.

Hussain Al-Ansari (10)
Edward Wilson Primary School, Westminster

Parents Have A Soul

Parents have a soul,
Whatever you do you must not break it,
If you do they might not refer to it,
If they pass, make sure to keep that soul,
Be sure to treat them with your full attention,
Make sure to always mention them in your future.

Zaynab Jannah (9)
Edward Wilson Primary School, Westminster

Summer

S unshine makes us joyful
U nderneath the clear blue sky
M aking sandcastles on the beach
M emories lasting forever
E ating ice cream all day long
R esting in the bright light sun.

Alaya Haque (6)
Edward Wilson Primary School, Westminster

I Am Brave

B etter than being scared
R ivers won't stop me
A little dragon won't hurt me
V olcanoes won't stop me
E verything is easy when I try!

Yasmin Saemh (6)
Edward Wilson Primary School, Westminster

A Boy

A mazing boy with
D azzling toys
Y awning in the morning
A lways in a hurry
A nd loves chicken curry
N o one is unique like me!

Adyaan Ali (6)
Edward Wilson Primary School, Westminster

A Journey Through The Galaxy

S un is the biggest
P luto is the most distant
A nd with all the others
C reates the solar system
E arth is our planet!

Diletta Vannone (6)
Edward Wilson Primary School, Westminster

Nature

The sky is blue,
And I am too.
The trees talk,
As I walk.
Everything is nature,
I love nature.

Sania Habib (7)
Edward Wilson Primary School, Westminster

Our House

A mazing view
H ouse, bright and big
M um makes
A pple pie
D ad eats.

Ahmad Al Salhani (7)
Edward Wilson Primary School, Westminster

Wildlife

A diamanté

Hedgehog
Spiky, prickly
Hiding, sleeping, playing
Garden, visitor, forest, hunter
Looking, fetching, scaring
Furry, hungry
Fox.

Casey Broadbent (6)
Greenside Primary School, Pudsey

Quick And Slow

A diamanté

Quick
Fast, speedy
Running, singing, skipping
Cheetah, rabbit, slug, tortoise
Queueing, walking, dancing
Calm, smooth
Slow.

Ophelia Meegan (5)
Greenside Primary School, Pudsey

Mummy And Daddy

A diamanté

Mummy
Nice, beautiful
Caring, cooking, washing
Becky, Mum, James, Dad
Vacuuming, playing, trumping
Strong, silly
Daddy.

Joss Mottram (5)
Greenside Primary School, Pudsey

My Mum And Dad

A diamanté

Mum
Pretty, kind
Cleaning, singing, kissing
Donna, Mummy, Dave, Daddy
Driving, laughing, cuddling
Fun, moustache
Dad.

Edie-Rose Horman (5)
Greenside Primary School, Pudsey

On The Earth

A diamanté

Sea
Cool, wet
Swimming, waving, splashing
Octopus, turtle, hedgehog, rabbit
Running, walking, looking
Warm, dry
Land.

Alfred Butterfield (5)
Greenside Primary School, Pudsey

The Sun And The Stars

A diamanté

Day
Bright, busy
Cycling, playing, learning
Sun, puma, owl, moon
Relaxing, dreaming, sleeping
Dark, peaceful
Night.

Valentina Haigh Del Rio (9)
Greenside Primary School, Pudsey

Bonfire Night

I can taste the gooey toasted marshmallows on my tongue.
I can taste the crunchy toffee apples.
I can smell the smoke from the bonfire.
I can smell mushy marshmallows toasting on the fire.
I can see the brightness of the fireworks.
I can see slippery and soggy grass.
I can feel the warmth of the sparkler in my hand.
I can hear the whole entire crowd screaming with joy.
I can hear the lovely sound of the bonfires crackling.

Jessica Marszol (7)
Hallglen Primary School, Hallglen

Bonfire Night

I can see flickering, floating lanterns.
I can see bright fireworks.
I can feel the cold on my nose and cheeks.
I can feel delicious food on my tongue.
I can hear bonfires crackling.
I can hear the emergency services racing to help.
I can taste crunchy toffee apples.
I can taste yummy barbecued food.
I can smell burning hot bonfires.
I can smell barbecues cooking tasty hot dogs.

Mudassir Khan (7)
Hallglen Primary School, Hallglen

Bonfire Night

I can see bright fireworks in the night sky.
I can hear loud explosions bursting from the rockets.
I can smell burning hot bonfires.
I can feel delicious food on my tongue.
I can taste yummy hot dogs.
I can hear children laughing.
I can smell smoky barbecues cooking tasty food.
I can see dark and spooky parks.
I can hear the emergency services racing to help.

Eloise Fraser (7)
Hallglen Primary School, Hallglen

Bonfire Night

I can see the slippery and soggy grass.
I can hear loud explosions.
I can hear bonfires crackling.
I can taste crunchy toffee apples.
I can taste delicious hot dogs.
I can see bright fireworks.
I can feel the cold on my nose and cheeks.
I can feel delicious food on my tongue.
I can smell fireworks exploding.
I can smell burning hot bonfires.

Harris Conroy (7)
Hallglen Primary School, Hallglen

Bonfire Night

I can taste crunchy toffee apples.
I can hear children laughing.
I can feel the cold on my nose and cheeks.
I can see hundreds of people watching.
I can hear people screaming with joy.
I can see bright fireworks.
I can taste delicious hot dogs.

Sophie Winton-Love (7)
Hallglen Primary School, Hallglen

Bonfire Night

I can taste toasted, gooey marshmallows.
I can hear loud explosions.
I can feel the cold on my nose and cheeks.
I can see bright fireworks.
I can smell burning hot bonfires.

Matthew Fyall (6)
Hallglen Primary School, Hallglen

Bonfire Night

I can taste steaming hot chocolate.
I can see bright fireworks.
I can hear loud explosions.
I can smell the burning hot fire.
I can feel the frost on my nose and cheeks.

Logan Neary (7)
Hallglen Primary School, Hallglen

Flames And Ice

A diamanté

Flames
Powerful, orange
Roasting, burning, scorching
Campfires, bonfires, frostbite, icicles
Slipping, dropping, melting
Shiny, cold
Ice.

Max Parkinson (6)
Jesmond Gardens Primary School, Hartlepool

Flames And Ice

A diamanté

Flames
Red, hot
Scorching, burning, roasting,
Campfires, s'mores, frostbite, icicles
Freezing, dropping, slipping
Cold, frosty
Ice.

Chloe Parkinson (10)
Jesmond Gardens Primary School, Hartlepool

Flames And Ice

A diamanté

Flames
Hot, powerful
Scorching, warming, roaring
Fire, embers, snow, icicles
Dropping, melting, freezing
Chilly, shiny
Ice.

Shay Malham (8)
Jesmond Gardens Primary School, Hartlepool

Flames And Ice

A diamanté

Flames
Powerful, hot
Cracking, roasting, burning
Fire, sparks, snow, frost
Slipping, freezing, dropping
Frosty, cold
Ice.

Leon Foster (11)
Jesmond Gardens Primary School, Hartlepool

Flames And Ice

A diamanté

Flames
Powerful, hot
Burning, roasting, roaring
Embers, fire, snow, icicles
Freezing, melting, dripping
Icy, chilly
Ice.

Callan Simpson (10)
Jesmond Gardens Primary School, Hartlepool

Day And Night

A diamanté

Day
Sunny, busy
Writing, playing, chatting
Sun, sunrise, sunset, stars
Twinkling, sleeping, snoring
Chilly, dark
Night.

Hollie Bradshaw (8)
Jesmond Gardens Primary School, Hartlepool

Day And Night

A diamanté

Day
Busy, sunny
Waking up, writing, playing
Sun, clouds, sunset, moon
Sleeping, snoring, dreaming
Dark, quiet
Night.

Octavia Trainer (7)
Jesmond Gardens Primary School, Hartlepool

Day And Night

A diamanté

Day
Bright, sunny
Writing, working, eating
Sun, sunrise, moon, stars
Reading, dreaming, sleeping
Quiet, dark
Night.

Daniel Shaw (10)
Jesmond Gardens Primary School, Hartlepool

Flames And Ice

A diamanté

Flames
Hot, red
Roaring, warming, burning
Fire, bonfire, frost, snow
Melting, slipping, freezing
Icy, chilly
Ice.

Emmie Pearce (7)
Jesmond Gardens Primary School, Hartlepool

Flames And Ice

A diamanté

Flames
Red, hot
Burning, warming, roaring
Fire, embers, snow, frost
Dropping, slipping, melting
Icy, cold
Ice.

Dean Malham (6)
Jesmond Gardens Primary School, Hartlepool

Haunted House

Pumpkins scattered across the ground,
And on top of a huge mound,
Is a haunted house!
Big ghosts and small ghouls,
And lots of salty slime pools,
Welcome to the haunted house!
Zombies and witches,
And wizard ditches,
Inside the haunted house!
Poltergeists and magic wands,
And stinky bog ponds,
And all over the haunted house!
So don't go in if you expect to come out alive!

Molly Conneely (8)
Marshgate Primary School, Richmond

Turtles

A kennings poem

Egg layer,
Beach washer,
Wave surfer,
Long liver,
Seabed explorer,
Coral inhabiter,
Fast swimmer,
Fish eater,
Shark avoider,
Caribbean coaster,
Slow blinker,
Shell user.

Charlie Sheldrick (8)
Marshgate Primary School, Richmond

Fat Cat

I am a fat cat, my name is Scratchy,
I like to be lazy and sit on the sofa.
I see my favourite owner, his name is Bucky,
I like to scratch his curtains and blame it on the dog.
I can smell milk and the stinky butt of our neighbour's cat.
I am a rebel with claws,
Sometimes I might scratch you.
I will break your favourite vase.
I can taste milk and rotten fish.

Eva Kuzmina (6)
Nelson Primary School, Ladywood

Sensory Skunk

If you startle a skunk, it will spray its musk,
A great stink that will linger a lot.

It stomps its front feet just to warn,
Lifts its tail and blasts anything in its way.

Some folk think that baths in the juice of tomatoes will wash away all of the smell.

But still, others say that vanilla, soap or mouthwash will do just as well.

Amna Abdulwhab (5)
Nelson Primary School, Ladywood

Nature In The Forest

Nature is everywhere,
Nature is everywhere you go.
Everything that lives and grows is nature,
Animals big and small,
Nature is plants that grow so tall.
Nature is beautiful in every way,
Wonderful, exciting,
And needs our care.
So listen, learn and do your part,
To keep nature,
Beautiful forever.

Amelia Vrapi (6)
Nelson Primary School, Ladywood

Sense Poem

I can hear, I can hear,
I can hear with my own ears.
I can see, I can see,
I can see with my own eyes.
I can smell, I can smell,
I can smell with my own nose.
I can taste, I can taste,
I can taste with my own mouth.
I can feel, I can feel,
I can feel with my own hands.

Namarikh Isak (6)
Nelson Primary School, Ladywood

My Senses

I can hear very well.
I can feel many things.
I can see very well.
I can smell everything.
I can taste the all food.

Marina Ago (5)
Nelson Primary School, Ladywood

Things I Like To Do

I can taste a leaf.
I can hear a bird tweeting.
I can feel petals.
I can smell a flower,
And I can see a butterfly.

Fareda Elshafey (5)
Nelson Primary School, Ladywood

The Parts Of My Body

I can see the window.
I can hear music.
I can feel my temperature.
I can smell food.
I can taste cake.

Karen Ireoluwa Taiwo (6)
Nelson Primary School, Ladywood

My World

I can see Mum.
I can smell flowers.
I can taste salt.
I can hear the wind.
I can feel the grass.

Sama Arjah (5)
Nelson Primary School, Ladywood

Animal Kennings

A kennings poem

Whisker wearer,
Cat dodger,
Cheese pincher,
Squeak maker,
Milk drinker,
Clock climber,
Milk stealer,
Squeak lover.
What am I?

Answer: A mouse.

Jaxon Appleby
Seahouses Primary School, Seahouses

Animal Kennings

A kennings poem

Milk stealer,
Cat dodger,
Wall hider,
Clock climber,
Milk drinker,
Whisker twitcher,
Cheese eater,
Squeak lover.
What am I?

Answer: A mouse.

William Armstrong (5)
Seahouses Primary School, Seahouses

Animal Kennings

A kennings poem

Cheese pincher,
Night sneaker,
Squeak lover,
Wall hider,
Cheese eater,
Cat dodger,
Milk stealer,
Clock climber.
What am I?

Answer: A mouse.

Daisy Winter (5)
Seahouses Primary School, Seahouses

Animal Kennings

A kennings poem

Worm lover,
Chip stealer,
Wing flapper,
Sky surfer,
Field lover,
Nest builder,
Feather spreader,
Sea floater.
What am I?

Answer: A gull.

Arthur Priestley (7)
Seahouses Primary School, Seahouses

Animal Kennings

A kennings poem

Tree climber,
Bamboo eater,
Tree lover,
Vine jumper,
Ground crawler,
Animal watcher,
Wood biter.
What am I?

Answer: A panda.

Jacob Rowe
Seahouses Primary School, Seahouses

Animal Kennings

A kennings poem

Cat dodger,
Night sneaker,
Squeak lover,
Wall hider,
Cheese eater,
Cheese hunter,
Milk drinker.
What am I?

Answer: A mouse.

Veronika Karpyshyn
Seahouses Primary School, Seahouses

Animal Kennings

A kennings poem

Ground jumper,
Australia lover,
Pouch sharer,
Leaf muncher,
Nose twitcher,
Koala watcher.
What am I?

Answer: A kangaroo.

Luella Campbell (6)
Seahouses Primary School, Seahouses

Animal Kennings

A kennings poem

Cheese eater,
Night sneaker,
Milk drinker,
Cat dodger,
Whisker twitcher.
What am I?

Answer: A mouse.

Sophie Bolam
Seahouses Primary School, Seahouses

Animal Kennings

A kennings poem

Cat dodger,
Cheese hunter,
Milk stealer,
Squeak maker,
Whisker twitcher.
What am I?

Answer: A mouse.

Reggie Stanwix
Seahouses Primary School, Seahouses

Animal Kennings

A kennings poem

Hole maker,
Scorpion eater,
Bird watcher,
Snake watcher,
Fast runner.
What am I?

Answer: A meerkat.

Jessica Owens
Seahouses Primary School, Seahouses

Animal Kennings

A kennings poem

Field hopper,
Burrow digger,
Carrot eater,
Nose twitcher,
Field lover.
What am I?

Answer: A rabbit.

Ava Thompson
Seahouses Primary School, Seahouses

Animal Kennings

A kennings poem

Squeak maker,
Cheese pincher,
Cat dodger,
Wall hider,
Squeak lover.
What am I?

Answer: A mouse.

Paige Douglas
Seahouses Primary School, Seahouses

Animal Kennings

A kennings poem

Den builder,
Night hunter,
Hen killer,
Tail flicker,
Person scarer.
What am I?

Answer: A fox.

Sienna Robinson (7)
Seahouses Primary School, Seahouses

Animal Kennings

A kennings poem

Meat lover,
Paw crawler,
Growl maker,
Animal hunter,
Space lover.
What am I?

Answer: A tiger.

Luke Liddell
Seahouses Primary School, Seahouses

Animal Kennings

A kennings poem

Den builder,
Lip licker,
Bird pouncer,
Cry maker,
Night hunter.
What am I?

Answer: A fox.

Alfie Neale
Seahouses Primary School, Seahouses

Animal Kennings

A kennings poem

Sand digger,
Toy chaser,
Meat eater,
Mess maker,
Field runner.
What am I?

Answer: A dog.

Nela Skibicka
Seahouses Primary School, Seahouses

Animal Kennings

A kennings poem

Feather spreader,
Beak pecker,
Claw dancer,
Squawk maker.
What am I?

Answer: A peacock.

Delilah Dunn
Seahouses Primary School, Seahouses

Animal Kennings

A kennings poem

Trunk waver,
Grass eater,
Water sprayer,
Stomp maker.
What am I?

Answer: An elephant.

Layla Kidd
Seahouses Primary School, Seahouses

Animal Kennings

A kennings poem

Puddle jumper,
Insect eater,
Rock sleeper,
Garden player.
What am I?

Answer: A frog.

Milana Filonenko (7)
Seahouses Primary School, Seahouses

Animal Kennings

A kennings poem

Roar maker,
Animal eater,
Crawling mover,
Land jumper.
What am I?

Answer: A tiger.

Leo Wood
Seahouses Primary School, Seahouses

Animal Kennings

A kennings poem

Egg eater,
Hiss maker,
Slithery mover,
Tongue licker.
What am I?

Answer: A snake.

Lailie Nakintije
Seahouses Primary School, Seahouses

Animal Kennings

A kennings poem

Hiss maker,
Egg layer,
Skin shedder,
Grass sneaker.
What am I?

Answer: A snake.

Axel McGilligan (6)
Seahouses Primary School, Seahouses

Ice Cream

I love ice cream, especially cherry.
It tastes sweet and tangy.
It smells fruity and very refreshing.
It feels cold and a little bit runny.
It looks very colourful, just like the rainbow.
Quick! I can hear the ice cream van coming,
It sounds like summer.
I love ice cream!

Michael-Junior Cameron (5)
South Rise Primary School, London

Foxes Are Funny

Foxes are red and white,
It is easy to see them in the light.
Even though they're known to bite,
I just might feed them some bread,
I hope I don't lose my head.
Foxes are silent, just like a mouse,
I hope they don't come back to my house.

Summer-Lilly Eldridge (6)
South Rise Primary School, London

Twister: The Hamster

Twister sleeps in the day,
Ester sleeps at night.
Ester wakes in the morning,
And gives Twister quite a fright.
By poking her finger at Twister,
Who bites her thumb really hard.
Ester now has a plaster,
She pulls her finger away a bit faster.

Romziyah Yusuff (5)
South Rise Primary School, London

Autumn Is Here

Leaves are falling.
Orange, red, brown.
I love finding helicopters on the ground.
I can't wait for Halloween.
Because I will get lots of sweets.
I am going to be a vampire for trick or treat.

Noah Assimeng-Boahene (6)
South Rise Primary School, London

Daily Life

I can hear birds singing and bushes rustling.
I can see beautiful flowers in my garden.
I can smell chips in my kitchen.
I taste yummy fish, delicious in my tummy.
I love stroking my lovely cat.

Asma Derder (5)
South Rise Primary School, London

Spring

Pink petals falling to the ground,
Bees flying around,
Birds are making tweeting sounds,
It makes me happy,
Because it is springtime.

Esma-Nur Sasmaz (6)
South Rise Primary School, London

Trip To The Beach

I can hear the sea.
I can feel the sand.
I can taste the food.
I can smell the water.
I can see the seaside.

Kaelin Pun (5)
South Rise Primary School, London

Autumn

Crisp leaves falling from the trees,
Red splotches dancing all around me,
Soaring high in the sky,
Gliding low to the ground,
Beautiful, even from a mile away.

The breathtaking colours
Entrancing even the weary of heart,
To be merry, to be joyful,
To be in awe of nature's art.

Dazzling under sunlight,
Twinkling under moonlight,
Flaunting its rare colours to the eye.
Impossible to fail to enchant
Even the weary of heart.

Autumn has arrived...

Aaron Singh (10)
St Aidan's Catholic Primary Academy, Ilford

Commander 64

There he was... Commander 64.
Indestructible and heroic,
Like no one you have ever seen before.

He had won many battles,
That he was famous for.
He had been on many tours,
But his last one was the worst, for sure!

Commander 64,
Fast approaching Planet 104.
He was wanting to attack,
Like he was in the Earth's core.

Valiant and courageous,
He fought a mighty war.
However nervous he was in battle,
He would not let it affect his thoughts.

The battle was extensive and tough,
Eventually, the aliens surrendered,
There was no hope for them at all.

Commander 64 ventured back into space,
Ready for duty, awaiting another call!

Sarab Sahota (10)
St Aidan's Catholic Primary Academy, Ilford

Queen Elizabeth II

Go peacefully, Your Majesty
With that courage we all knew
With your favourite colour, blue!
Everyone was upset about you.

You gave everyone a charming smile
And you gave everyone a delightful day
You shocked the world
Seventy years, you helped the country
In all different ways.

Now we have a king that will take over
Rest in peace, Your Majesty!

Deivan Virdee (10)
St Aidan's Catholic Primary Academy, Ilford

Christmas

C arol singing in the frosty air
H olly wreaths are everywhere
R emember to leave your stocking out
I t is true that you will shout
S anta Claus is coming to town
T o be honest, the reindeer are brown
M ince pies are baking in the oven
A ngels come down in like a dozen
S o now you've learnt your lesson.

Eunice Bonanga (10)
St Aidan's Catholic Primary Academy, Ilford

Can You Guess The Animal?

I can see in the dark,
And hate animals that bark.
I can jump very high,
And hate it when my owner says, "Bye."
I love to eat mice,
But have never tried rice.
I love drinking milk,
And sometimes lie on silk.
Can you guess what I am?

Answer: A cat.

Pedro Ekemezie (10)
St Aidan's Catholic Primary Academy, Ilford

Paris

P aris is made out of love
A n amazing and outstanding place to be
R adiant stars light up the blackened sky
I t is a phenomenal sight to witness
S o much love is spread around Paris, it is incredible. It is a joyful place to be.

Destiny Ugwu (10)
St Aidan's Catholic Primary Academy, Ilford

The Bakery

I can see the desserts,
I can smell the mouth-watering treats.
I can hear the bell ring,
That means it's time to eat.
I can feel the warmth from the oven,
Rising in the air.
I can taste the chocolate filling,
That makes me want to share!

Safiyya Moosa (10)
St Aidan's Catholic Primary Academy, Ilford

London

L ights flash by on the late-night buses
O ver the River Thames and back
N o one about on the streets
D reams turn into unicorns and fairies
O nly six people left on the bus
N ew things to experience.

Isabella Jackman (10)
St Aidan's Catholic Primary Academy, Ilford

The Starry Night

I flew up high
In the starry
Night sky!
Then I saw
A magical light.
I thought it was
nothing, so I
Took a closer
Look...
It was a star
Floating up
High!

Ariana Zaman (10)
St Aidan's Catholic Primary Academy, Ilford

Lovely Thoughts

I like to see my lovely, brave Mum and Dad,
They are great at making me feel glad.
Fluffy cats and furry dogs,
They're great, that's true,
But they're nothing compared to my toy fennec fox, who makes me feel happy,
With her spectacular, giant ears and adorable eyes,
That takes away my cries.
At Nan-nan's house, there is a cute cat, Lola,
Her silly meow is so delightful,
I almost forgot, there is also scrumptious vanilla ice cream!

Sarai Mallett-Odeyale (7)
St Mary's Lewisham CE Primary School, Lewisham

My World

I like to see,
Shimmering, sparkling gold shining through the window,
A bright glittery star sparkling in the night sky,
The colourful, glittering rainbow in the sky.

I like to smell,
Yummy, crispy bacon sizzling in the pan,
Sweet, tasty candyfloss twisting on a stick,
Squishy, soft sponge cake baking in the oven.

Ananya Vijithan (7)
St Mary's Lewisham CE Primary School, Lewisham

Mixed Senses

I like to see,
The beautiful, clear sky,
Freshly boiled rice dancing in the pot.

I like to taste,
Cooked, edible snails,
Tasty Belgian chips that you can't stop eating,
Spicy, grilled peri-peri.

I like to touch,
Warm, soft cats when nobody is passing by,
Squishy, stretchy rubber bands.

Elyas Yahya (7)
St Mary's Lewisham CE Primary School, Lewisham

I Like...

I like to see,
Blue whales swimming on TV,
Giant jellyfish floating in the sea,
Bloop, a type of whale eating one thousand fish.

I like to hear,
A small baby crying,
Clapping, shouting noises,
Big, creepy squid making weird noises.

Eddy Charles (7)
St Mary's Lewisham CE Primary School, Lewisham

I Like...

I like to see,
A beautiful, colourful rainbow,
The golden, shining sun,
My huge family.

I like to hear,
Loud, wonderful music playing,
Cute, cuddly babies giggling,
A large, hard fountain giving water.

Haja Jalloh (7)
St Mary's Lewisham CE Primary School, Lewisham

I Like...

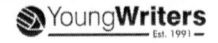

I like to see,
My kind, helpful friends,
The beautiful, pretty sun,
The beautiful, glittering solar system.

I like to hear,
Quiet, calming music,
A loud, noisy ice cream van,
A small baby laughing.

Temi Adelaja (8)
St Mary's Lewisham CE Primary School, Lewisham

Great Senses

I like to see,
A big sandy beach,
Yummy, tasty sweets,
Big crashing waves.

I like to hear,
Loud, wet rain,
Fast, zooming cars,
The cute giggles of a baby.

Lucian Stefan Eftimie (7)
St Mary's Lewisham CE Primary School, Lewisham

I Like...

I like to see,
A sparkly rainbow,
My special teddies,
Lots of special teachers.

I like to taste,
A small kiwi,
A small apple,
Lots of big strawberries.

Sandra Aguilera (7)
St Mary's Lewisham CE Primary School, Lewisham

At London Zoo

First, I saw the camels with their humps on their back,
Then I saw the white bear, then I saw the black,
Then I saw a horse eating its straw,
Then I saw a grey wolf with mutton in his maw,
Then I saw a sloth hanging on a branch,
Then I saw the monkey and it smelt awful!

Megan Ivanov (9)
Stonesfield Primary School, Stonesfield

The Moon, The Rain And The Snow

A kennings poem

Moon:
Night lighter,
Sun's sister,
Magic bringer,
Stars' mother,
Tide controller,
Dark starter,
Day over.

Rain:
Water giver,
Soft splatter,
Cold splashes,
Pitter-patter,
Life giver,
Cat teaser,

River maker,
Wet drencher.

Snow:
Soft blanket,
Perfect flakes,
White Christmas,
Boxing Day,
Fun maker,
Traffic stopper,
Cold weather,
Big adventure.

Iris Maroney (10)
Stonesfield Primary School, Stonesfield

What Am I?

A kennings poem

Sky spinner,
Window passer,
Glowing plummeter,
Magic holder,
Wish giver.
Frost bringer,
Icicle maker,
Magic sorcerer,
Joy holder,
Letter writer,
Second mother,
Christmas time,
Carol singer.
What am I?

Imogen Doucas (10)
Stonesfield Primary School, Stonesfield

What Am I?

A kennings poem

Night hisser,
Slimy critter,
Fanged creature,
Scaly green,
Sneaky ninja,
Bear strangler,
Deer eater,
Rabbit cruncher,
Tree climber.
What am I?

Answer: A snake.

Billy Hulusi (10)
Stonesfield Primary School, Stonesfield

What Am I?

A kennings poem

Fire holder,
Bone wearer,
Magic bearer,
Bone stomper,
(I mean I am walking bones),
Night walker,
Fright bringer,
Face melter,
(I mean I don't have a face).
What am I?

Daniel Hunt (9)
Stonesfield Primary School, Stonesfield

What Am I?

A kennings poem

Night hunter,
Fish hunter,
Sharp teeth,
Super swimmer,
Ocean owner,
Hungry predator,
Deep swimmer,
Mega eater.
What am I?

Answer: A shark.

Tegan English (10)
Stonesfield Primary School, Stonesfield

Guess This!

A kennings poem

Quick traveller,
Hot boiler,
Track runner,
Steam puffer,
Coal eater,
Whistle blower,
Station stopper.
Who or what am I?

Answer: A steam train.

Abel Stuart (9)
Stonesfield Primary School, Stonesfield

A Force Of Nature

A kennings poem

Storm bringer,
Eerie howler,
Tree feller,
Air power,
Hair blower,
House shaker,
Rain lasher,
Thunder maker.
What am I?

Answer: The wind.

Leo Turner (10)
Stonesfield Primary School, Stonesfield

Can You Guess?

A kennings poem

Best friend,
White hair,
Perfect girl,
Always there,
Nice lighter,
Bendy noodle,
Head scratcher,
Little sister.
Who am I?

Answer: Mimi.

Aaliyah Gregory (9)
Stonesfield Primary School, Stonesfield

What Am I?

A kennings poem

Tongue launcher,
Rain sleeper,
Lily pad watcher,
Spawn bringer,
Pond leaper,
Bug eater,
Tadpole teacher.
What am I?

Answer: A frog.

Isaac Smyth-Medina (10)
Stonesfield Primary School, Stonesfield

What Am I?

A kennings poem

Furry fisher,
Great swimmer,
Paw thudder,
Deep growler,
Tree rubber,
Scent leaver,
Unstoppable eater.
What am I?

Answer: A bear.

Rocco Hulcup (10)
Stonesfield Primary School, Stonesfield

What Am I?

A kennings poem

Super sleeper,
Good hunter,
Paw padder,
Stealthy hider,
Easy killer,
Hyper animal,
Stripy attacker.
What am I?

Answer: A tiger.

Leland Edwards (9)
Stonesfield Primary School, Stonesfield

What Am I?

A kennings poem

Slippy hunter,
Fish eater,
Pipe lover,
Leaf eater,
Mussel muncher,
Darting killer,
Egg layer.
What am I?

Answer: A fish.

Daniel (10)
Stonesfield Primary School, Stonesfield

What Am I?

A kennings poem

Tail wagger,
Bone cruncher,
Fast digger,
Soft cuddler,
Fur wearer,
Fast runner.
What am I?

Answer: A dog.

Rowan Ball (11)
Stonesfield Primary School, Stonesfield

What Am I?

A kennings poem

Jungle swinger,
Forest leaper,
Fruit gatherer,
Play fighter,
Banana eater.
What am I?

Answer: A monkey.

Freya Harris (10)
Stonesfield Primary School, Stonesfield

What Am I?

A kennings poem

Night creeper,
Moon howler,
Tree scratcher,
Brave alpha,
Forest walker.
What am I?

Answer: A wolf.

Ellis F (10)
Stonesfield Primary School, Stonesfield

In The Night

A kennings poem

Scary time,
Time goes,
Bats watch,
Black time,
Stars come,
Waking up,
Work time,
No driver.

Samuel Smith (9)
Stonesfield Primary School, Stonesfield

The Sunken Shipwreck

- **S** unken old boat
- **H** idden at the bottom of the deep, dark, salty sea
- **I** nside the shipwreck, there was an orange patterned fish
- **P** retty, glistening gold treasure
- **W** here can you find treasure?
- **R** otten, brown wood on the yellow sand
- **E** ven the heavy, grey anchor had split out
- **C** ould this be a puzzling mystery?
- **K** ept as part of history.

Tayabung Rai (7)
The Bemrose School, Derby

Treasure

T owering pieces of gold littering the underwater
R ock around by the rustling waves
E legant, shining and beautiful to behold
A quatic habitat created
S potty octopus squirting
U nderwater fishes swimming
R ushing around the golden treasure
E verywhere is beautiful and shining.

Princess Adetoyese (6)
The Bemrose School, Derby

Twinkling Treasure

T he shimmery treasure is under the sea
R aging, arching waves
E nchanted treasure
A rching waves
S tarlit sea
U nderwater shiny treasure
R eally amazing sight
E verywhere is bright.

Amy Nirmal (6)
The Bemrose School, Derby

My Super Senses

I can taste sweet orange chocolate.
I can smell yucky Marmite.
I can feel cotton wool.
I can see lots of people in line.
I can hear the sizzling rain stick.

Jonas Full (5)
Willington Prep School, Wimbledon

My Super Senses

I can taste minty chocolate.
I can hear a noisy rain stick.
I can feel fluffy cotton wool.
I can smell yucky coffee.
I can see monkey bars in a playground.

Angus Timlin (5)
Willington Prep School, Wimbledon

My Super Senses

I can smell yucky Marmite.
I can taste orangey chocolate.
I can hear a sizzling rain stick.
I can feel soft cotton wool.
I can see lots of people.

Alexander Hohlfeldt (6)
Willington Prep School, Wimbledon

My Super Senses

I can taste chocolate.
I can hear a sizzling rain stick.
I can smell Marmite.
I can feel fluffy cotton wool.
I can see a flying bird.

William Parkhouse (5)
Willington Prep School, Wimbledon

My Super Senses

I can taste minty chocolate.
I can hear the shaking rain stick.
I can feel fluffy cotton.
I can see children.
I can smell coffee.

Edward Lu (5)
Willington Prep School, Wimbledon

My Super Senses

I can hear a sizzling rain stick.
I can taste chocolatey chocolate.
I can smell sour Marmite.
I can feel fluffy cotton wool.

Matthew Plant (5)
Willington Prep School, Wimbledon

My Super Senses

I can hear sizzling beads.
I can feel cotton wool.
I can see a house.
I can smell coffee.
I can taste minty chocolate.

Reuben Stern (5)
Willington Prep School, Wimbledon

My Super Senses

I can taste chocolate.
I can smell Marmite.
I can see children.
I can feel cotton wool.
I can hear a rain stick.

Charlie Livesey (5)
Willington Prep School, Wimbledon

My Super Senses

I can hear the rain.
I can feel cotton wool.
I can see a line.
I can smell yucky coffee.
I can taste chocolate.

Maxim Russell-Omaljev (5)
Willington Prep School, Wimbledon

My Super Senses

I can taste chocolate.
I can hear rain.
I can feel cotton wool.
I can smell yummy coffee.
I can see children.

Tom Fell (5)
Willington Prep School, Wimbledon

My Super Senses

I can hear sizzling.
I can feel cotton.
I can see a playground.
I can taste orange chocolate.

Edward Jones (5)
Willington Prep School, Wimbledon

Friendship

F riends encourage me
R eal friendship will last forever
I like playing with my friends
E veryone needs a friend
N obody likes to be sad or alone
D o nice things to help your friends
S hare your opinions with your friends
H elp and respect each other
I nterested in what a friend says
P eacefully solve problems with friends.

Rishi Sivathasan (6)
Yeading Infant & Nursery School, Hayes

Calming Butterfly

B eautiful butterfly comes out of the cocoon,
U p it flies in the blue sky.
T ravelling high to find sweet fruits,
T asty tangerine - mmmm, yummy!
E very flower looks so bright,
R ainbow colours, a lovely sight!
F *lutter, flutter*, go her pretty wings,
L oving the sound of the birds singing.
Y ou make me feel calm!

Khushleen Kaur Bhogal (6)
Yeading Infant & Nursery School, Hayes

Vehicles

V ans can be huge or small, but
E lectric ones are the best of all!
H eavy lorries are passing by
I n the highway's traffic jam
C ars can run on diesel or petrol
L oaded with shopping from Tesco
E lectric cars are great for the environment but it's a
S cooter I choose when I go to school.

Saim Hussain (6)
Yeading Infant & Nursery School, Hayes

Love Unicorns

U nicorns are like horses with a horn
N ow I wish I could have one
I would ride it to the moon and stars
C ome with me and we can be magical superstars
O nly people who believe will see the sparkle
R ainbows are slides and clouds are like candyfloss
N ow you can see why I love unicorns.

Riyana Chudasama (6)
Yeading Infant & Nursery School, Hayes

Bubbles

B lue, red, yellow, green and purple
U p they float with the wind and go home
B ig, colourful, floating bubbles
B lowing bubbles is lots of fun
L ight and airy, high they fly
E veryone wants to pop one!
S oapy and watery, the bubbles float away.

Taimur Nizam-Uddin (6)
Yeading Infant & Nursery School, Hayes

Zorawar

Z ebras are my favourite animal
O vals are my favourite shape
R eading is my favourite subject
A dorable is what my mummy calls me
W ashing dishes is fun to do
A n astronaut is what I want to be
R unning is what keeps me fit.

Zorawar Buttar (6)
Yeading Infant & Nursery School, Hayes

Save Earth

S top pollution
A ct now
V aluable planet of ours
E arth is precious

E arth is our priority
A nimals need to be saved
R educe, reuse, recycle
T ogether, we can
H ealthy Earth, happy Earth.

Harleen Gill (6)
Yeading Infant & Nursery School, Hayes

Holidays

H ot day in the summer
O ver at the seaside
L ots of fun
I love the beach
D ays are fun
A nd I eat ice cream
Y um, yum yoghurt
S weet ice lollies.

Harjot Singh (6)
Yeading Infant & Nursery School, Hayes

The Magical Rainbow Glitter

M ake wishes come true
A nd the skies are blue
G litter going everywhere
I like bears
C ats are soft
A nd they play in the loft
L ots of magical stories.

Aya Al-Hulu (6)
Yeading Infant & Nursery School, Hayes

Playing With My Friends

When we go outside,
We go to the park,
Okay, it is wonderful outside,
Then we play football,
And there are people sitting on the bench,
And kids are playing on the slide.

Ranveer Singh (7)
Yeading Infant & Nursery School, Hayes

Apple

A pples are red and yummy
P ineapples are not an apple
P ointed pencil and sharpener
L ove from Akshaana
E lephants have long trunks.

Akshaana Parthipan (6)
Yeading Infant & Nursery School, Hayes

House

H ome is where the heart is
O therwise, it's just a house
U s as a family
S tay together
E specially with your loved ones.

Maisa Azad (6)
Yeading Infant & Nursery School, Hayes

Summer Fun

S unshine on my face
U nderwater swimming
M aking lemonade
M any long walks
E arly sunrise
R unning in the park.

Eshan Rekhi (6)
Yeading Infant & Nursery School, Hayes

Israr

I ce on the mountains
S pider on the wall
R abbit in the grass
A ntelope is running
R oses are in the garden.

Israr Ahmed Shinwari (7)
Yeading Infant & Nursery School, Hayes

Happy

H aving a great time
A ll my friends are here
P laying with toys
P ainting and colouring
Y ou can join in!

Harleen Jaspal (6)
Yeading Infant & Nursery School, Hayes

Play

P laying in the park
L aying on the grass
A ll my friends are playing on the slide
Y ou can run in the park.

Sahib Gill (6)
Yeading Infant & Nursery School, Hayes

Star

S hining bright at night
T winkling in the night sky
A s pointy as a cactus
R unning around in a circle.

Shay-Anne Kirk (7)
Yeading Infant & Nursery School, Hayes

Angry Crocodile

A ngry
C rocodile
R an
O ver
S ome
T iny
I nsect
C olonies.

Abhishaek Rajeswaran (6)
Yeading Infant & Nursery School, Hayes

Shining Sky

S hining in the sky
T winkling the whole night
A s bright as a light
R eally looks so white.

Jasreet Khabra (7)
Yeading Infant & Nursery School, Hayes

Farm

F armers produce vegetables
A nd give us food
R ain helps them a lot
M y hobby is farming.

Akai Nithiyaramnarayanan (6)
Yeading Infant & Nursery School, Hayes

The Life Of A Book

I have all your wisdom
You feed me it through ink
You shove me in a box
Because you don't care about me a wink!

I have lots of empty pages
So you don't run out of space
You rip them out though
It's a very common case!

When you fill me up
My future is the bin
You chuck me in there
It's such an awful sin!

When I'm in the landfill
A thought occurs to me
I might be yours again
Maybe after tea!

Jessica Dymond (10)
Yelvertoft Primary School, Yelvertoft

Bonfires

B oom, whoosh, whizz!
O utside, the fireworks sparkle all over the city
N ovember the 5th is a very special night for everyone
F ireworks everywhere, they're so bright at night
I nside the houses, they celebrate with beer and wine
R emember, remember, the 5th of November
E nding the night is a sad time
S pecial night for everyone, I must say.

Reuben Flavell (10)
Yelvertoft Primary School, Yelvertoft

Bonfires

B *oom, whoosh, whizz!*
O utside, the fireworks sparkle and fizz
N ovember the 5th is a special night
F ireworks everywhere, they're so bright
I nside the houses, people celebrate with beer and wine
R emember, remember, the 5th of November
E nding the night is a sad time
S pecial night for everyone, I must say!

Niamh McElfatrick (9)
Yelvertoft Primary School, Yelvertoft

Trick Or Treat

I wander at night but only one night,
I say with my friends, "Trick or Treat?"
Everyone in these houses throws sweets at me,
I walk to all the houses in the village,
I spook the lives out of everyone,
But make sure I am filled to the brim.
Who am I?

Answer: A trick or treat pumpkin bucket.

Elijah Elliott (9)
Yelvertoft Primary School, Yelvertoft

The Halloween Glow

I can be all sorts of looks.
Usually, I'm scary but sometimes I'm not.
I'm orange and green, I'm also glowing.
Usually, people see me but just walk on by.
I don't stay forever, eventually, I die.
The fire inside me makes me what I am.
What am I?

Answer: A Jack-o'-lantern.

James Fleming (9)
Yelvertoft Primary School, Yelvertoft

Autumn Pumpkins

P umpkin spice tastes so nice
U nder trees, conkers are falling
M inute mice foraging for food before hibernation
P retty leaves are falling from the trees
K ids running around in woolly hats
I nside houses, fires are burning
N o sign of leaves returning to green.

Kirin Kaur Madhar (9)
Yelvertoft Primary School, Yelvertoft

Something In The Ground

I'm in a store, or in the ground,
Sometimes in your mouth with a frown.
Occasionally, I can have a face,
And I'm mashed up on your dinner plate.
Sometimes butter is on me,
I'm brown and round, that's how you see me.
What am I?

Answer: A potato.

Eva Newhouse (9)
Yelvertoft Primary School, Yelvertoft

Pumpkin Spice

Lots and lots of fun,
Lots of fun carving pumpkins,
Walking on the leaves.

I'm a dead spirit hunting your soul,
I'm spooky and scary,
And I have a goal.

So beware, beware,
Your kids will be gone,
I will always have my fun.

Tessa Clews (10)
Yelvertoft Primary School, Yelvertoft

Autumn Whiskers

Haiku poetry

Soft angel purring,
Nice and comfy by the glow,
Sleeping all day long.

I lap up my milk,
I flick my tail up gently,
Everyone loves me.

Soft angel purring,
Please don't ever let me go!
Lovely, don't you know?

Natalie Ritchie (10)
Yelvertoft Primary School, Yelvertoft

Water Bottle

I'm in a backpack,
Night and day,
When I'm on a dinner plate,
It's hip, hip, hooray!
Empty and lonely,
I feel so blue,
Full of water,
I'm happy and true,
When I'm spinning
I go with the flow, being cool.

Tommy Starkey (10)
Yelvertoft Primary School, Yelvertoft

Bubble Trouble

My liquid can be blue, green or red,
And my sounds can be *splish, splash or pop!*
My smell can sometimes be regretful,
But my taste, please, just don't!
What am I?

Answer: A cauldron.

Grace Micklewright (11)
Yelvertoft Primary School, Yelvertoft

Halloween

Haiku poetry

Walking on the leaves,
The crunchy toffee apples,
Nice, warm candyfloss.

Nice, warm hot chocolate,
Chilling by the nice, warm fire,
Keeping nice and warm.

Bethany Shaw (9)
Yelvertoft Primary School, Yelvertoft

A Spooky Time

I turn from white to orange.
I come in all sizes.
I am scary but sweet.
I am tasty to eat.
I go in a pie.
What am I?

Answer: A pumpkin.

Elouise Shakespeare-Luck (10)
Yelvertoft Primary School, Yelvertoft

Autumn Days

A diamanté

Conkers
Shiny, smooth
Dropping, cracking, opening
Squirrel, acorns, seeds, autumn
Collecting, scurrying, tumbling
Miniscule, enticing
Acorns.

Matilda Kington (10)
Yelvertoft Primary School, Yelvertoft

Autumn

A diamanté

Squirrels
Furry, cute
Cheeky, nasty, red
Mice, hedgehogs, seeds, birds
Spiky, cute, cuddly
Big, majestic
Hedgehog.

Flynn Armstrong (9)
Yelvertoft Primary School, Yelvertoft

Coffee Mug Night

Hot, steamy, nice and warm,
Ready to drink in the autumn storm,
I live up on the countertop,
Ready to drink steaming hot.

Esme Carter (9)
Yelvertoft Primary School, Yelvertoft

YOUNG WRITERS INFORMATION

We hope you have enjoyed reading this book – and that you will continue to in the coming years.

If you're the parent or family member of an enthusiastic poet or story writer, do visit our website **www.youngwriters.co.uk/subscribe** and sign up to receive news, competitions, writing challenges and tips, activities and much, much more! There's lots to keep budding writers motivated!

If you would like to order further copies of this book, or any of our other titles, then please give us a call or order via your online account.

Young Writers
Remus House
Coltsfoot Drive
Peterborough
PE2 9BF
(01733) 890066
info@youngwriters.co.uk

Join in the conversation!
Tips, news, giveaways and much more!

YoungWritersUK YoungWritersCW youngwriterscw